AMY NG

Amy Ng was born in Australia, grew up in Hong Kong and is based in London. She trained and worked as a historian before turning to playwriting. Her debut play *Shangri-La* premiered at the Finborough Theatre in July 2016. Her radio play *Tiger Girls* will be broadcast 17 July 2018 on BBC Radio 4. She is under commission to the Royal Shakespeare Company, Belgrade Theatre Coventry, Yellow Earth Theatre, and feminist theatre company Dangerous Space. She was recently named to the BBC New Talent Hotlist 2017.

Amy is also the author of *Nationalism and Political Liberty* (Oxford University Press).

Other Titles in this Series

Amy Ng

ACCEPTANCE

NICK HERN BOOKS

London

www.nickhernbooks.co.uk

A Nick Hern Book

Acceptance first published in Great Britain as a paperback original in 2018 by Nick Hern Books Limited, The Glasshouse, 49a Goldhawk Road, London W12 8QP

Acceptance copyright © 2018 Amy Ng

Amy Ng has asserted her right to be identified as the author of this work

Cover image: istockphoto.com/Digital21

Designed and typeset by Nick Hern Books, London
Printed in the UK by Mimeo Ltd, Huntingdon, Cambridgeshire PE29 6XX

A CIP catalogue record for this book is available from the British Library

ISBN 978 1 84842 736 5

Acceptance was first performed at Hampstead Theatre Downstairs, London, on 2 March 2018. The cast was as follows:

BIRCH	Teresa Banham
MERCY	Debbie Korley
ANGELA	Jennifer Leong
BEN	Bo Poraj
Director	Anna Ledwich
Designer	Frankie Bradshaw
Lighting	Elliot Griggs
Sound	Alexandra Faye Braithwaite

Acknowledgements

Thanks to all the people and organisations who contributed along the way:

Dr. Michael Jellinek, Fin Kennedy, Neil McPherson, the Finborough Theatre, Nic Wass, Greg Mosse, Ping Choon Ng, Ian Nicholson, Matt Schmolle, Drayton Hiers, Yellow Earth Theatre, Arts Council England for funding the initial R&D, Rebecca Manson-Jones, Margaret Glover, and the many actors who read for me at different stages.

I am very grateful to the whole team at Hampstead Theatre, in particular Ed Hall, Greg Ripley-Duggan and Will Mortimer, for backing the play. Heartfelt thanks also to director Anna Ledwich and the cast who together interrogated and improved the play during the rehearsal process.

A.N.

For Michael

Characters

ANGELA CHAN, *student from Hong Kong, seventeen
    years old*
MERCY JONES, *black British junior admissions officer at
    Eliot University, thirty years old*
BIRCH COFFIN, *acting Dean of Admissions at Eliot
    University. Boston Brahmin background. Fifties*
BEN COHEN, *Associate Professor of Music and diversity
    expert at Eliot University. Jewish, liberal. Fifties*

Time

The present.

Setting

The admissions office of Eliot University, an elite university in
Boston, Massachusetts.

The bar of a concert hall.

Music

Bach's 'St Matthew Passion' is a key reference here, especially
Judas's aria 'Give Me Back My Jesus' (the 'Unforgiven' aria),
and 'Have Mercy Upon Me' (the 'Mercy' aria). At moments of
great stress, Angela hears the arias as an aural hallucination.

*This text went to press before the end of rehearsals and so may
differ slightly from the play as performed.*

Scene One

*The voices of Eliot University applicants read fragments
from their personal essays, which accelerate, crescendo, and
overlap, as if competing for attention.*

A. I am

B. I am

C. I am

D. I am

A. I am Mexican-American.

B. I am Texan.

C. I am a citizen of the world.

D. I am stateless.

A. I am British.

B. I am European.

C. I am Jewish.

D. I am Muslim.

A. I am an all-American tennis champion.

B. I am Native American.

C. I come from six generations of Eliot men.

D. I come from a hearing-impaired lesbian family.

A. My parents are Vietnamese refugees.

B. My grandmother's a Holocaust survivor.

C. My great-great-grandmother was a slave.

D. My ancestors were Native Americans wiped out by white
settlers in Boston.

A. I admire Martin Luther King

B. I admire Hillary Clinton

C. I admire Buddha

D. I admire Mandela

A. I love the light at dawn

B. I love the smell of paint

C. I love David Bowie

ANGELA *enters. She is a shadowy figure in the dark.*

ANGELA. 'We hold these truths to be self-evident, that all men are created equal, that they are endowed by their Creator with certain unalienable Rights, that among these are Life, Liberty and the pursuit of Happiness.' I cried when I first read the American Declaration of Independence. I cried that there were rights I never knew I possessed. All my life I had been their performing monkey, their trophy-winning child prodigy, playing Bach and Mozart on demand like so much tinkling elevator music. But in my dreams I could hear another music, something vital and urgent, bloodied, embryonic, and I knew I could give form to these charging, surging energies – if only I were in the land of the free...

Scene Two

November. Evening.

Eliot University Admissions Office.

ANGELA, *in school uniform, waits nervously. She cradles a violin case.*

BIRCH, *immaculate in twin-set cashmere and pearl earrings, enters.*

BIRCH. Good evening. I'm Birch Coffin, the acting Dean of Admissions.

ANGELA. Angela Chan. Nice meeting you.

BIRCH (*looking at violin*). I hope you were not expecting members of our music faculty to be here tonight.

ANGELA. No, no, I'm not auditioning… I was going to a concert tonight and…

BIRCH. You're playing at a concert tonight?

ANGELA. No. I just bring it along. For luck.

ANGELA *barricades herself with the violin case on her lap.*

BIRCH. Optimistic to book a concert for the evening of your interview.

ANGELA. Sorry. I thought – 5 p.m. interview – I'd definitely make it to Symphony Hall by seven thirty.

BIRCH. For the Peter Sellers/Simon Rattle 'Matthew Passion'?

ANGELA. Yes.

BIRCH (*half apology*). We've been absolutely snowed under… I had tickets too.

BIRCH *takes a seat.*

ANGELA *hovers awkwardly.*

Do sit down.

ANGELA *sits.*

Pause.

Do you know why we invited you here?

ANGELA (*beat*). To discuss my application.

  ANGELA *takes out a folder.*

  I brought a copy. I've also done some of the additional essays.

BIRCH. How diligent.

ANGELA. The questions are so very interesting! 'An intellectual experience that has meant the most to you.' I love that you ask not just about the experience but about the 'meaning'. I wrote about 12/8 time in Bach and the blues. The 'Erbarme Dich – Have Mercy Upon Me' aria in 'St Matthew Passion' is in 12/8 time. (*Sings it, beating out the time.*) It's about Peter's remorse, after he's denied Christ –

BIRCH. And the 12/8 beats are the tears rolling down Peter's cheeks. We have thirty-seven thousand, four hundred and fifty-one applicants. Thirty-seven thousand, four hundred and fifty-one applications. To be read by thirty-six admissions officers. We can't possibly meet with every applicant. Do you know why we have asked you to come here?

ANGELA. I am honoured that you should take time from your busy schedule to meet with me.

BIRCH. Why are you here?

ANGELA. I don't know.

  Pause.

BIRCH. There are certain irregularities in your academic career.

ANGELA. Irregularities? (*Pause.*) I have straight-As from all the schools I've attended.

BIRCH. *All* the schools. It is unusual to attend three schools in four years.

ANGELA. I was at the Trinity Girls' School in Hong Kong for ten years. I then won a scholarship to the Performing Arts High School in New York City, after which I transferred to the Boston Music School here.

BIRCH. The Performing Arts High School is one of the best music schools in the country. Visiting musicians from Juilliard, the New York Philharmonic, give lessons there. Why would an aspiring musician leave… voluntarily?

ANGELA. I want to focus more on composition. My Boston school is better for that.

BIRCH. We ask for two recommendations from teachers who know you well.

ANGELA. I have two recommendations from my current teachers.

BIRCH. Who have known you for two months. Why didn't you ask the teachers in New York for recommendations?

ANGELA (*beat*). I am not in touch with them.

BIRCH. We need those recommendations to complete your application.

ANGELA. I'll try…

BIRCH. Is there a reason why they wouldn't recommend you?

ANGELA *hears the 'Unforgiven' aria and starts strumming on her arm.*

So. Additional essays. Did you try this: 'Unusual circumstances in your life'?

ANGELA. No.

BIRCH. What about this one – 'The Eliot Honour code declares that we "hold honesty as the foundation of our community". Please reflect on a time when you or someone you observed had to make a choice about whether to act with integrity and honesty.'

ANGELA. I am honest! I've told the truth!

BIRCH. Okay. My task is to pick suitable candidates for Eliot. That will contribute to our community. Because you see, every single one of our thirty-seven thousand, four hundred and fifty-one applicants is outstanding in some way. Academic aptitude. That's a given. Olympic athletes. Musical prodigies. We get them all. We are looking for Character. People who demonstrate Leadership. Who give back to Society. A Community where people feel safe. Where they can trust that their friends, their fellow students, are people of integrity.

ANGELA. You think I'm not – a person of integrity?

BIRCH. Did I say that?

ANGELA. So you believe I'm – a person of integrity.

BIRCH. You tell me.

ANGELA. I'm not a 'delusional liar' or a 'fantasist' or –

ANGELA shivers uncontrollably and strums on her arm.

The music crescendos.

BIRCH. Are you alright?

ANGELA. Fine. I'm fine. Sorry. If I had known I would have prepared… you know. Steel myself. I didn't – I expected – something different.

BIRCH. What did you expect?

ANGELA. The usual… Academics. Extracurriculars. What do you want to be twenty years from now? What are your strengths? What are your weaknesses?

BIRCH (*pleasantly*). Alright. We can certainly do that. What are your weaknesses?

ANGELA. I used to play like a child prodigy rather than with real artistry. But I'm trying –

BIRCH. Character weakness.

Pause.

ANGELA. I'm not good at saying 'no'. Like… my roommate. She's very nice. But she likes turning up her music loud. (*With distaste.*) Taylor Swift. Beyoncé. I stuff in my ear plugs but she doesn't notice. She opens the windows, I put on my shawl, and my sweater, and a woollen hat, but *still* she doesn't see. And I – can't – just tell her.

The music is loud, frenetic and distorted.

ANGELA's fingers execute vibratos on her arm.

BIRCH. What are you playing?

ANGELA. Playing?

BIRCH. You're playing something specific – a phrase, a melody.

ANGELA. It's nothing. Autopilot.

BIRCH. Can you play it?

ANGELA. Play?

BIRCH. On your violin.

ANGELA. No!

BIRCH. No?

ANGELA. The case is empty.

BIRCH. You carry an empty violin case.

ANGELA. My violin might get crushed during rush hour in
the trains.

BIRCH. Your case looks sturdy enough to me.

ANGELA. I can't risk damaging my violin!

Pause.

BIRCH. Let's try strengths, shall we? What are your strengths?

ANGELA. Music.

BIRCH. Character strengths.

ANGELA. Bach composed for the greater glory of God. But his
music is a knot of suffering and beauty and violence.
Sometimes I feel I'm on the verge of solving it – if I could
only cut through, I would understand how to go on – how we
musicians can go on. How not to give in to despair...

BIRCH. And that's a strength? I'm sorry. Are you equating your
struggles as a musician with his? A man who lived at a time
when life expectancy was approximately thirty. Ten of his
children died in childhood.

ANGELA. I didn't mean it that way.

BIRCH. Come on. From your guts. What are your strengths?

Long pause.

ANGELA. I think…

I'm quite…

I can be…

I have…

BIRCH. You're thinking too much.

Scene Three

Next day. Morning.

Eliot University Admissions Office.

MERCY *packs up her laptop. She takes off her business suit jacket to reveal a 'Black Lives Matter' T-shirt and slips off her heels for trainers.*

ANGELA *enters.*

ANGELA. Excuse me, I'm looking for Ms Mercy Jones.

MERCY. I'm Mercy.

ANGELA. Angela Chan. I'm one of the applicants. May I ask you some questions about scholarships for ethnic minorities –

MERCY. I'm on my way to the march in DC.

ANGELA. Oh – sorry.

ANGELA *slumps and turns to leave.*

MERCY. I really don't know how helpful I can be. Asians are no longer considered under affirmative action. Sorry.

ANGELA. Oh.

MERCY. But I'm almost certain all students whose families earn less than sixty-five thousand dollars are eligible for a full ride at Eliot. You'd better double check with the financial-aid office though.

ANGELA. Okay.

MERCY. Even families who earn up to two hundred thousand dollars are eligible for some financial aid. Which means that most applicants can get support.

ANGELA. That's... good.

MERCY. What do your parents do?

ANGELA (*beat*). They're surgeons.

MERCY (*angrily*). So why are you looking for a scholarship?

ANGELA. My family's cut me off.

MERCY. Oh. I'm sorry. Why?

ANGELA. It's... Long story –

    MERCY *glances at her watch.*

MERCY. I'm late for my plane to DC. Look, basically you need to prove that your family has disowned you, or that you have to stay away for your safety. Social-worker reports, police reports, you got anything in writing?

ANGELA. Writing?

MERCY. Like a letter from your parents disowning you.

ANGELA. I have an email...

MERCY. Good, good. So how are you supporting yourself now?

ANGELA. I have a music scholarship from the Hong Kong government. But it runs out this year.

MERCY. An international student?

ANGELA. I know it's more difficult for us.

MERCY. America First America First. I'm British. Took me six months for them to sort out my visa though we have eleven in-house lawyers at Eliot. As for financial aid – forget it.

ANGELA. Oh.

MERCY. Don't despair. Where there's a will... Did you say music? We've got a fantastic music scholarship here – full ride at Eliot, plus funding for touring nationally and internationally – I don't know all the details but my colleague Birch Coffin runs it. Why don't you make an appointment with her.

ANGELA. I've met… I don't think…

MERCY. You've met Birch?

ANGELA. Yes.

MERCY. And you don't think – what?

ANGELA. I'm not applying for the music scholarship.

MERCY. Why not? You must be good –

ANGELA. I don't think Dr Coffin wants me to apply…

MERCY. She said that?

ANGELA. –

MERCY. I know Birch can be a bit frosty but surely. Leave this with me. Angela – Chan? Right?

ANGELA (*nods*). Thank you.

Scene Four

Same day. Evening.

MERCY *has just arrived back from DC. Her 'Black Lives Matter' T-shirt is stained and her jeans are ripped.*

BEN *enters, looking dapper in blue blazer and khakis.*

MERCY. Professor Cohen!

BEN. Ben.

MERCY. Ben… Ben. Feels weird.

BEN. We're colleagues now.

MERCY. Old habits.

BEN. 'The student repays the teacher poorly by remaining a student.'

MERCY. Quoting Nietzsche is so *undergraduate, Professor…*

BEN *enfolds* MERCY *in a big bear hug.*

BEN. Mercy Jones! You haven't changed. Sorry I wasn't here to welcome you at the beginning of the semester.

MERCY. That's alright. I know you can't resist swanning around, soaking up the applause –

BEN. Swanning? I beg your pardon.

MERCY. Peacocking?

BEN. Penguin-ing, maybe. Not many peacocks in Peru.

MERCY. Peru? I thought you were in Venezuela.

BEN. Oh. That. Completely overrated.

MERCY. But the Venezuelans are the gold standard for increasing access to classical music –

BEN. I think we do a better job in New York City.

MERCY. You've done such a fantastic job at Juilliard!

BEN. Fifteen per cent of last year's intake was African American or Hispanic! (*Beat.*) How's your wrist?

MERCY. Better. But it's never going to heal enough to...

BEN (*beat*). I'm sorry.

MERCY. Blessing in disguise, really. I never told you this, but at Tanglewood I realised I'd never be the best... I won't settle for being a second- or third-rate harpist.

BEN. Then I'm sorry I recommended you for Tanglewood.

MERCY. No. It's good to find out early – I think I'd gotten so far only because of the rarity value – a black harpist!

BEN. You'll make your mark on the world another way. I'm not worried about that. (*Beat.*) Work visa all sorted? They've got eleven in-house lawyers at Eliot, you know –

MERCY. Yes. I have a one-year work visa.

BEN. Did you get a room in College?

MERCY. Yes.

BEN. Are they decent?

MERCY. Yes they're great.

BEN. All your stuff arrived? Did you get Eliot to pay for it all?

MERCY. Yes and yes –

BEN. How was the march?

MERCY. Amazing! One of the best days in my life! To see this sea of black faces, empowered, dignified, strong –

BEN. And their pale stale white fellow travellers?

MERCY. A sea of black faces with some white froth on top –

BEN (*putting his hand over his heart theatrically*). Froth! We're froth!

MERCY. People were cheering from both sides as we closed in on the White House. They formed a human chain, keeping the hecklers away. We were joined by the women's march, the Dreamers' march, the trans-in-military march, a real rainbow coalition –

BEN (*singing*). 'Someday we'll find it, the rainbow coalition, lovers and dreamers and me.' Love Kermit. The voice of idealism with a sense of irony.

MERCY. This is why I came to America.

MERCY *takes out a bottle of champagne and two glasses. She pours some and hands* BEN *a glass.*

BEN. To your American dream!

MERCY. To the man who will change the face of university admissions in America!

BEN. I'm just a consultant to the admissions office. To the new Diversity Officer at Eliot University!

MERCY *clinks glasses with* BEN.

MERCY (*conspiratorially*). Birch is just the *acting* Dean of Admissions.

BEN. Whoa. Stop right there. I'm just the new kid on the block. I'm not even sure I *want* – all these carefully calibrated personal essays with just the right proportion of surmountable adversity and positive thinking. Personal my ass! Come on! You know my truth-serum interview question? 'You have fifty grand to consume tonight – what would you do?'

MERCY. I'd donate it to Black Lives Matter.

BEN. *Consume*, all of it, so no giving away to charity, no buying of property, no investment…

MERCY. I'd travel to the Himalayan foothills to visit a recently discovered matriarchy –

BEN. You have one night. You'd still be on the plane when your fifty grand turns back into a pumpkin.

MERCY. Oh.

BEN. Not that easy now, is it? An X-ray into the soul… I get such interesting answers. So what would you do?

MERCY *(beat)*. I'd spend it on an Alexander McQueen dress.

BEN *(beat)*. Seriously? Mercy! Wow!

MERCY. Oh I know I don't look the fashion type…

BEN. Where did that come from?

MERCY. Alexander McQueen held his early fashion shows right around where my cousins lived. In Shoreditch. It wasn't all gentrified then. I remember visiting one half-term and walking past this church and suddenly these girls came out – Brick Lane girls, tough, lesbian – McQueen loved his tough lesbian chicks, and they were utterly transformed by his dresses, like dark angels…

BEN. That's the second best answer I've ever heard.

MERCY. What was the best?

BEN. You don't need to escape into someone else's fashion fairytale.

MERCY takes a framed photo from her bag and places it on BEN's desk.

What's this?

MERCY. Ruby Bridges. The first black girl who fought segregation in schools –

BEN. I know who Ruby Bridges is. A bit on the nose, don't you think?

MERCY. We're throwing down the gauntlet to the Establishment –

BEN. Birch is not 'the Establishment'. She's someone we need to work with.

MERCY. For fuck's sake! Her dad's name is on this building! Just because she has a vagina –

BIRCH *enters*.

BEN. Birch!

BIRCH. Ben. Am I interrupting?

MERCY. I'll make tea.

MERCY *exits rapidly to put the kettle on*.

BIRCH. I trust you are settling in.

BEN. Yes. Thank you. I already know most of my colleagues in the music department, so I'm sure I'll feel very welcome.

BIRCH. I shall introduce you to the other thirty-three admissions officers later. We have a hot-desk system, and many officers choose to work from home.

BEN. I hear we have a record number of applicants.

BIRCH. Thirty-seven thousand, four hundred and fifty-one at last count.

BEN. Sorry to have left you all in the lurch for the first two months.

BIRCH. Not at all. How was Peru?

BEN. Fantastic. I was trying to find out how classical music can help overcome trauma amongst indigenous people in the Andean mountains.

BIRCH. Admirable.

BEN. It's not so different from bringing music to inner-city kids.

BIRCH. Yes. We are very glad to have your expertise this year.

MERCY *returns*.

BEN (*grins*). If I can sell classical music to those kids, I can sell Eliot?

BIRCH *does not smile*.

I know there's a lot less financial aid available this year...

MERCY. That reminds me – there was an applicant. A musician. She asked me about ethnic-minority scholarships, and I urged her to apply for the music scholarship. She seemed to think you wouldn't welcome that though.

BIRCH. And which applicant is that?

MERCY. Angela Chan. A misunderstanding, I'm sure. I can't imagine you discouraging an applicant.

BIRCH. Angela Chan accused her music teacher of rape.

MERCY. What?

BIRCH. The allegations were not substantiated.

MERCY. How do you know?

BIRCH. I called the Performing Arts High School in New York City when I saw Angela didn't have any recommendations from them.

MERCY. Rape cases are notoriously hard to judge –

BIRCH. True. Still, she might get in on the music scholarship. We must assess the risk.

MERCY. What risk?

BIRCH. She falsely accused a teacher of rape, or she could be a kitchen cabinet.

MERCY. A *what*?

BIRCH. Full of porcelain, 'boo', and everything shatters.

MERCY. Is it Eliot policy not to admit anyone with potential mental-health issues?

BEN. I'll get the – ah –

BEN *exits to make tea*.

BIRCH. It is Eliot policy to admit students who will contribute to the community, not destabilise it.

MERCY. We want the best. Angela's a brilliant student, world-class musician – she's been loaned a Stradivarius by a Hong Kong bank, I mean. Wow.

BIRCH. Wow?

MERCY. She must be good.

BIRCH. *Nothing* is an automatic ticket to Eliot – not an Olympic gold medal, not a Stradivarius. Every year there are at least a dozen technically flawless Asians playing the same virtuosic pieces – the competition gets more tedious by the year.

MERCY. She doesn't even want to apply for the music scholarship.

BIRCH. Is that right? Well, in that case… Goodnight.

BIRCH *exits*.

BEN *enters with three cups of tea*.

BEN. I still remember the Proper English Way of brewing tea – I hope.

MERCY. 'Technically flawless Asians' – was it just me or is she borderline racist –

BEN. It's an observation. You know that joke about Jewish parents making their kids learn music to train nimble fingers – you know, future neurosurgeons –

MERCY. And misogynistic to boot! The consensus amongst experts is that ninety-seven per cent of rape allegations are true.

BEN. 'The quality of *Mercy* is not strained' –

MERCY. Birch knew Angela was too visible with her Stradivarius, otherwise she would have buried her under the other thirty-seven thousand, four hundred and fifty applications.

BEN. 'It droppeth as the gentle rain from heaven' –

MERCY. She's completely a tool of the White Anglo-Saxon Patriarchy!

BEN. She is a product of her upbringing and class and era. It's a long game we're playing. We need Birch to cooperate. We do not need you stampeding around like a bull in a China shop –

MERCY. Full of fragile porcelain, 'boo' and it shatters!

BEN. I need you, Mercy. Look at me. Pale, male, middle-class, middle-aged. I need you for legitimacy, authenticity, integrity. The last thing I want is for you to leave the country because Birch won't sponsor you for a visa extension.

MERCY. So – what? I'm to kowtow?

BEN. Our mission is to increase diversity at Eliot. We need more African Americans, Hispanics, Native Americans, Polynesians. We do not need more Asians. They're over-represented already.

MERCY. Our mission is not to hunt down rare minorities like trophies. Our mission is to create a level playing field no matter what your race, gender or class –

BEN. Absolutely. The Holy Grail – a critical mass of brilliant minorities. But then go find them, Mercy. Don't get distracted by a case which no doubt is tragic but hardly representative –

MERCY. The assumption that any woman of colour is sexually available is very representative of –

BEN. Rape is not an affirmative-action category! (*Beat.*) Sorry. That was insensitive.

Pause.

MERCY. Professor Cohen... Ben. You're too good. You assume other men are like you. The things I've seen – what I've had to put up – let's just say you were the only professor who was interested in my mind, not my...

BEN. Thank you. But would I dare mentor another bright young student these days? One doesn't even dare shut the door any more when teaching, or go the extra mile for a student, stay after hours, listen to them pour out their hearts over coffee or drinks.

MERCY. Women *know* when a man's being friendly or nurturing or when there's coercion behind the charm. They absolutely know.

BEN. Do they, Mercy? Do they really?

Scene Five

Two weeks later. Early morning.

Admissions office.

MERCY *and* ANGELA *are sharing a bagel breakfast.*

MERCY. Sorry it's been a while. I was on the road. I just got back from a boarding school for Native Americans in Wyoming. Hopefully one or two of them will apply.

ANGELA. Thank you for taking the time to see me.

MERCY. Have you got the email?

ANGELA (*takes out a printout*). This is from my mother. She cancelled my plane ticket home for my dad's fiftieth birthday, and told me to stay away.

MERCY. Not enough. We need something showing a more definitive break.

ANGELA. I don't have anything else. They've not called or emailed or texted for a year.

MERCY. It's unfair. I know. But they have to set the bar high, otherwise any student could stage a fight with their family then claim financial support. But this means we're back to the music scholarship I'm afraid.

ANGELA. I don't have a violin any more.

MERCY. But... (*Looks at the violin case.*)

ANGELA. It's empty.

MERCY. Why?

ANGELA. The bank took the Stradivarius back.

MERCY. Is that because of your... case?

ANGELA *(beat)*. Yes. The bank took it back because I was no longer a good ambassador for their brand.

MERCY. I assume your parents cut you off for the same reason?

ANGELA. Yes.

MERCY. I know it happens – honour and shame and all that – but if I had a daughter and this happened to her...

ANGELA. I understand my parents. They're afraid everyone will look down on our family.

MERCY. You have done nothing shameful! You're a survivor! They should have been there for you, every step of the way. Did you have to go through the trial alone?

ANGELA. There was no trial. My parents refused to press charges. There was an internal hearing organised by the school. My parents did not attend.

MERCY. How old are you?

ANGELA. Eighteen in a week.

MERCY. So in a week you can press charges without their consent.

ANGELA. I don't want to press charges.

MERCY. Angela. You *need* to press charges. Stop him doing this to some other young woman –

ANGELA. He left for another country.

MERCY. So he fled the law. So he thinks he got away with it. We've got to name and shame him! Who was it?

ANGELA. I signed a confidentiality agreement.

MERCY. You did what? Why?

ANGELA. They said if I signed, they would help me with my visa. They said if I signed, they would keep my case confidential, it wouldn't appear on my record, it would not affect my college applications.

MERCY. And you believed them.

ANGELA. Does it affect my application?

MERCY. What do you think, Angela?

ANGELA *starts tapping on her arm.*

You win the music scholarship and nothing – not your New York school, not the other admissions officers – can stop you from entering Eliot.

ANGELA. I can't.

MERCY. The other competitors won't have a Stradivarius either.

ANGELA. It doesn't matter anyway. Dr Coffin says I need two recommendations from my New York school. I called my biology and history teachers. But they don't dare.

MERCY. I'll sort it out with Birch. You shouldn't be penalised for their cowardice.

ANGELA. They're afraid of mobbing... of trolls.

MERCY. Were you trolled, Angela?

ANGELA. My diary was subpoenaed for the hearing. They got a Chinese teacher at my school to translate it. Extracts were posted anonymously on the school e-bulletin board.

MERCY. That's despicable. (*Beat.*) But listen, if you blow them away at the scholarship competition, in ten years – Carnegie Hall!

ANGELA. I can't play.

MERCY. Sprained ligament? You *have* to jump on it right away – believe me, I speak from experience – a specialist physiotherapist –

ANGELA. No. I haven't played since he...

MERCY. Listen to me, Angela. You've been so brave. You picked up that phone. You called the police. You accused your rapist. All I'm asking for is a little more of that courage... It's just a block. A – phobia. I was terrified of spiders. I couldn't even stand looking at those white flowers with the spindly petals. But the zoo ran this programme called 'My Friend the Spider'. And I took it. I won't claim I love spiders now, but I'm cool with them, I'm in control.

ANGELA. 'My friend the – professor'?

MERCY. I'm sorry, I didn't mean – And I understand why you signed that NDA. But I need to know more, Angela. All I – all any of us knows is that you accused a teacher of rape, but he got off anyway. Which means – you know how that looks –

ANGELA. 'Delusional nymphomaniac', 'fantasist', 'vengeful', 'hysterical'…

MERCY. Let's change the narrative. (*Beat.*) Who was it?

ANGELA. I signed the non-disclosure –

MERCY. Which arguably they've breached. Which means you're not bound – is it someone well known? I don't care who he is, he can't do anything to you –

ANGELA. I can get a scholarship to the Royal Northern College of Music in Manchester. My former Hong Kong teacher is now a professor there.

MERCY. You want to go to England? Brexit England?

ANGELA. 'America first, America first.'

MERCY. Americans are fighting back, in the courts, on the streets, in City Hall, in universities – sanctuary cities, whole sanctuary states! In Britain, it's just a lot of handwringing in the *Guardian*. I was born in Yorkshire and still get asked if I'm from Nigeria. I've been here three months, and people accept me as almost American.

ANGELA. Almost. It's always almost.

MERCY. There were nine black undergrads in my year at Oxford. Nine of us. Flying under the radar, trying so hard to fit in. Fucking baa baa black sheep amongst all the Oxford tossers – my tutor never discussed my ideas, just circled, in red, every misplaced comma. Then suddenly, this American visiting professor, descending from on high like Mary Poppins, and he was *interested*, he *engaged* with my ideas, he *saw* me as a human being worthy of respect. He helped me get this job. Look at me! A gatekeeper at Eliot University! I get to choose who becomes America's elite, the world's elite! I get to change the world.

ANGELA (*violently*). I am not the world! (*Shrinking*.) I'm sorry.

MERCY. You have a gift. Use it. Whatever mental block that's keeping you from playing – blast through it. Upload those audition samples. Write that application. And for God's sake, don't write another mini-dissertation on Bach's 12/8 time signature. You were supposed to write about something deeply meaningful and personal – that's why it's called a personal essay –

ANGELA. The first time it… happened… afterwards I took the subway back to school. It was one of those open-air stations on a bridge over the road. I watched the steam rising from the manholes in the pavement below, as train after train pulled in and out again. I felt my body had turned to stone, that I couldn't possibly ever move again, except to drop down straight into the oncoming traffic. Then a busker started playing blues on the violin – so sad, but glowing, like dark hot sweet potato pie. A blues gospel, with a walking bass in 12/8 time. Like Bach's 'Mercy' aria… And I could move again.

MERCY. Was your busker playing a Stradivarius?

ANGELA. Probably not.

MERCY. QED – it's the violinist that matters. Not the violin.

The lights dim. The chorus of applicant voices start up again.

A. I want

B. I want

C. I want

D. I want

A. I want to find kindred spirits

B. I want to be amongst poets and dreamers

C. I want to work with the best in the world

D. I want friends. I want to stop feeling like the nerdy geeky outsider.

ANGELA. I burnt my boats. I took a leap of faith across the oceans. I laid myself wide open to America. I met a teacher. For the first time my body became a vessel of music, vibrating in my thighs, in my womb, along my spine, exploding in my blood. I was plugged into an electric current which runs through all true musicians, breathing together, sweating together, falling silent together, climaxing together. Pinocchio became a real boy. Music became flesh. (*Smiles beatifically.*) Incarnation.

Scene Six

December. Evening.

The admissions office.

BIRCH *is working through applications.*

MERCY *enters in a stunning evening dress.*

BIRCH. That's a beautiful dress.

MERCY. Thank you. (*Beat.*) It's an Alexander McQueen.

BIRCH. It's exquisite. Special occasion?

MERCY. I'm going to the Christmas drinks at the music department.

BIRCH. With Ben?

MERCY (*beat*). Yes.

    Sound of a car. MERCY *starts.*

BIRCH. That's not him. Ben's car was snowed in this morning.

MERCY. Oh of course.

BIRCH. He's charming. Ben.

MERCY. Yes.

BIRCH. Over the years, I've met many professors like him. Charismatic. With many female followers.

MERCY. About the Angela Chan case –

BIRCH. What about it?

MERCY. Angela signed a non-disclosure agreement, in return for the promise that her case would be kept confidential. Especially with regard to college applications. Did you know that?

BIRCH. I did not know that. How did you find out?

MERCY. Angela told me.

BIRCH. Have you been meeting her in private?

MERCY. We claim to be the best university in the world. Shouldn't fact-finding and inquiry be at the heart of whatever we do?

BIRCH. It is completely inappropriate to blur the line between admissions officer and activist!

MERCY. It says in *your* guidelines that 'an admissions officer should judge each applicant holistically'.

BIRCH. 'Holistically' means from all sides. Not just taking her word against everyone else's.

MERCY. From all sides. Not just taking the institution's word.

BIRCH. Angela's application would have been a lot stronger if she'd written about the case from her point of view. When I saw that Angela had attended the Performing Arts School without obtaining a single letter of recommendation, alarm bells rang. It could mean cheating, or drug use, or a breakdown. I've known their college counsellor for at least ten years. So I asked her – *confidentially*. And she told me – *confidentially* – what happened.

MERCY. So if I put in a Freedom of Information Act request for Angela's case records, would you read it? For a *holistic* view?

BIRCH. Why are you so obsessed with this case?

MERCY. You've never been groped?

BIRCH. Really, Mercy!

MERCY. Oh my God. You've never been groped.

BIRCH. Mercy, this conversation is completely inappropriate and distasteful –

MERCY. You've never been groped because your daddy's name is on this building. But what about all those women without your privilege?

BIRCH. Not everything can be reduced to white privilege.

MERCY. That's not what I'm saying. But perhaps you don't appreciate how misogynistic this system can be

BIRCH. Oh I appreciate it all right. I've been here thirty years. I've been *acting* dean of three different departments. Ben's seconded for one year to the admissions office. He's being paid forty per cent more than me.

MERCY. But your dad –

BIRCH. Father would have approved. He opposed co-education at Eliot.

MERCY. Then why stay? If I kept on being passed over I'd leave… Or is there no life outside Eliot for a descendent of the founding fathers?

BIRCH. I once hoped to be an Episcopalian priest.

MERCY. Oh. What happened?

BIRCH. Then I became an administrator in my father's university.

Pause.

MERCY. I know it seems unfair but – consultants always get more than regular employees. We're the whitest university in the Ivy League and Ben increased diversity at Juilliard by about three hundred per cent

BIRCH. And isn't it just so typical of Eliot to promote a white male diversity expert over a woman?

Pause.

Knocking at the door. They both ignore it.

MERCY (*without conviction*). He's Jewish.

BIRCH. It's different for your generation. You're young. Black. Female. You could well become Dean of Admissions here one day. You don't need Ben and you certainly don't need to spend two months' salary on a dress to impress him. Don't join his harem, will you?

MERCY. I'm sorry?

BIRCH. Metaphorically speaking.

MERCY. I can assure you I've never felt even the hint of anything inappropriate...

BIRCH. I'm glad to hear that.

MERCY. I *know* when a man has ulterior motives, and I would appreciate it if you stopped *insinuating* – groundless...

BIRCH. Maybe you're not his type.

Knocking on the door.

MERCY *opens the door.*

ANGELA *enters.*

ANGELA. I'm sorry I know it's late but the wifi failed and the deadline's today I brought the music application –

MERCY. Thanks, Angela. Leave it on my desk. I really need to –

MERCY *leaves swiftly, terrified of losing her composure.*

BIRCH. I thought you weren't applying for the music scholarship.

BIRCH *takes the application, opens the envelope and scans through it.*

ANGELA. Did Ms Jones tell you – I couldn't get the two recommendations...

BIRCH. You've put down a Bach aria for your chamber music piece.

ANGELA. Yes.

BIRCH. Unconventional choice.

ANGELA. It's not against the rules. The violin is not an accompanist, but an equal partner to the singer. Yehudi Menuhin once said –

BIRCH. That the 'Have Mercy Upon Me' is the most beautiful piece of music ever written for the violin.

ANGELA. Yes!

BIRCH. And still. I don't recall any violinist ever choosing an aria for a competition.

ANGELA. This aria is about Peter, about mercy. Forgiveness. But there's a different one, Judas's aria, that always gets in the way. 'Give me back my Jesus!' Please turn time back, please unmake the past, please mend what is broken, please restore what I've lost – the singer on his knees, supplicating, the G-major violin solo dancing, dazzling, vicious, interrupting the singer, cutting him off 'shut up shut up shut up I don't care what you say go kill yourself burn in hell forever'. Peter and Judas. Both sinned. Both begged for forgiveness. One was rejected. One was accepted. Why is that? Two thieves were crucified with Christ. One was rejected, one was accepted. Why is that?

The music fades.

I set out to play 'Mercy', but I hear the 'Unforgiven' instead.

BIRCH. And you think coming to Eliot would silence the 'Unforgiven'?

Pause.

ANGELA. It's my birthday today. No one's called. No one sent a card. Rape is like Aids. But if I were at Eliot... *Everyone* knows Eliot. My relatives back in the village. My illiterate grandmothers. My neighbours, the hairdresser, the fruit seller. Eliot's the only name which can turn lead into gold. I come to Eliot, and everyone will want to know me again.

BIRCH. They won't forget.

ANGELA. Maybe they won't bring it up.

BIRCH (*beat*). Judas and Peter. One was forgiven. The other
could not receive forgiveness. 'Give me back my Jesus!'
Turn time back, unmake the past, mend what is broken,
restore what I've lost. Judas is stuck in the past, in an endless
loop of remorse and guilt. He's lost all hope that he can be
acceptable again. Peter, on the other hand, abandons himself
to mercy, and finds acceptance. (*Beat*.) Happy birthday.

Scene Seven

January.

Admissions office.

On the table, an opened Fedex parcel with a folder inside.

BEN. The pastors, the priests, the sports coaches – who else?

MERCY (*distracted*). Hairdressers?

BEN. Hairdressers. Why not. The barber shops. The nail salons.
Hell, the tattoo parlours. Anywhere, everywhere, I want you
to spread the word. We're not just going to do a recruit and
dump. No more will we accept a dropout rate of eighty-two
per cent for inner-city kids. Once they step foot on campus,
they'll get wrap-around support. They'll get a weekly one-
on-one tutorial, like at Oxford, so no one falls between the
cracks. They'll get graded pass/fail only in the first two
years, until they catch up with the rest. We'll have
counsellors, and community centres; the canteen will serve
soul food and Mexican food – is Puerto Rican food fairly
similar to Mexican? Mercy? Mercy.

MERCY. Sorry, Ben. It all sounds great.

BEN. What's wrong?

MERCY. Just a migraine.

> BEN *takes* MERCY*'s hand and starts pressing the
> acupuncture point on the web between her thumb and
> index finger.*

What are you doing?

BEN. Acupressure. I've never felt such a blocked meridian.

MERCY *savours the moment.*

MERCY. Ouch.

BEN. Sorry.

MERCY. How come you know acupressure?

BEN. I used to date a Japanese acupuncturist. She could play the body like a violin –

MERCY *twists away.*

I know – too much information. The love-life of the middle-aged... She used to say, 'If it doesn't flow, it hurts.' Your energy's blocked. What's happening?

MERCY. Thanks. It's almost gone.

BEN. What's wrong, Mercy?

MERCY *hesitates, then indicates the folder.*

What's this?

MERCY. Open it.

BEN *opens it and scans through the first page.*

BEN. What is it? –

MERCY. This is the Angela Chan case.

BEN *(beat)*. How did you get a hold of this?

MERCY. I requested Angela's case records under the Freedom of Information Act.

BEN. How is that even possible? Wouldn't she have been a minor?

MERCY. They've blacked out the names and anything that could identify rapist or victim.

BEN. We have thirty-seven, four hundred and fifty-one applicants. Seven per cent of those are ethnic minorities. We have ten days to round up more. Every minute you spend on her case is time lost on another candidate. Think of all those brilliant minority candidates you could be discovering, wooing, encouraging –

MERCY. Ben, this is the case that everyone's trying to bury. If Angela had been a victim of any other crime, if she'd been mugged, or had her identity stolen, been lynched by racists, made to work in a sweat shop, deported, you would totally be on her side.

BEN. The indigenous people of the Andes have a ritual called *pampachanakuy*, where former perpetrators and victims agree to forget aspects of the past. We're talking horrific stuff here – massacres, mass rape, cannibalism. But they know something that we in the West don't know with our 'more truth equals more healing equals more reconciliation' mantra – that a statute of limitations on past crimes is just as important for the *victims...*

MERCY. How can I look Angela in the eye and just tell her to forget?

BEN. One bird with broken wings. Thirty-seven thousand, four hundred and fifty-one candidates.

MERCY. Do you know who he is?

BEN. Who?

MERCY. The rapist.

BEN. No! Why would I know that?

MERCY. He was a visiting teacher who came once a week to teach their best students. They've blacked out his professional affiliation, but Juilliard staff teach at the Performing Arts High School –

BEN. And at the special music school, and at Horace Mann, and at Stuyvesant and even all the way up to Connecticut. I didn't keep track of all my colleagues' side hustles for money.

MERCY. But were there rumours?

BEN. There're always rumours. It's every teacher's nightmare. You work so hard to awake a spark of desire – for beauty, for understanding – and you find yourself with something like fatal attraction. Students get close to inspiring teachers. We shouldn't always criminalise desire.

MERCY. I walk through Copley Place every Sunday on the way to church. Where the Pradas and the Armanis and the Alexander McQueens of the world spend millions, millions to awaken desire – for goods I'd never be able to afford. And if I acted on my desire it'd be called shoplifting, or burglary; in the nineteenth century I'd have ended up in a penal colony, in the eighteenth century executed –

BEN. Point taken. But Mercy – don't underestimate how much pressure a gorgeous young girl –

MERCY. She's a schoolgirl.

BEN. Yeah. They're the worst. Tsunami waves of hormones, amoral, egocentric, flinging themselves kamikaze fashion at any available –

MERCY. Angela's not like that.

BEN. Oh really? Look at this. (*Indicating the report.*) There were four alleged incidents. If it was rape, why didn't she call for help after the first one?

MERCY. Imagine you were a foreigner, or a woman of colour, would you automatically look to the police for help?

BEN. She didn't call the police. She called a child-abuse hotline. I have a friend who volunteers at the Samaritans. Do you know how many pervs they get who just call to masturbate? And slumber-party pranksters – desperate sounding twelve-year-olds who go on and on about the horrific abuse they're suffering – except it ends with giggles and laughter and a sudden hang-up! Ten per cent of the calls to the Ebola hotline in Liberia were pranks! This Angela Chan was twenty flight hours away from home. Probably a bit socially inept like so many of these Asian prodigies. New kid on the block, and she wanted some human sympathy and attention – don't we all? So she made up this whole story, just for a half-hour's temporary intimacy with some phone counsellor, never dreaming it'd be reported to the police and traced back to her.

BIRCH *enters*.

Oh hi, Birch.

Pause as BIRCH *surveys the scene.*

Mercy here went ahead and requested some extracurricular reading.

MERCY. The Angela Chan case.

BIRCH. Your FOI request?

MERCY. As per our previous discussion. The police report, and the transcripts of the hearing.

BEN (*turning to the back of the file*). Hang on. Did you see this? She wore Opium.

BIRCH. At the hearing?

BEN. These are extracts from her diary.

MERCY. Stop!

BEN. You requested these records, Mercy.

MERCY *grabs hold of the folder and shows* BEN *and* BIRCH *a photo of Angela's diary.*

MERCY. This is her diary. Her pink Hello Kitty diary with a little heart-shaped lock.

BIRCH. Goodness.

MERCY *turns another page and shows them scanned pages from* ANGELA's *diary. The purple inked writing is in Chinese.*

MERCY. Probably written with a scented felt pen. This is a young girl's diary! You can't just read it! It's such a violation…

BEN. This is evidence. It's in the public domain.

MERCY. They were translated by a Chinese teacher. A colleague of the rapist's. Does that sound like an impartial translation to you, Birch? It's misleading! Ripped out of context!

BIRCH. How do you know?

MERCY. Angela told me.

BIRCH. Do you have independent verification of the translator's identity? Have you consulted a Chinese speaker on the accuracy of the translations?

MERCY. They were plastered all over the school e-bulletin board! Tell me that's not an inside job.

BEN (*reads*). 'Today I have a private lesson with "blank". I spray Opium by YSL on my hair, my throat, my cleavage, my thighs. I wear my Victoria Secrets black-lace bra and panties and spray them too.' That's just classic – Opium! Casts Little Miss China-Doll in a whole different light, doesn't it?

MERCY. It's just perfume! Birch. The judge appointed for the hearing was a Performing Arts High School alumnus. He used the 'beyond all reasonable doubt' rather than 'preponderance of evidence' standard to judge the allegations. What do you think of that?

BIRCH (*beat*). I think it sounds like some basic errors were made.

MERCY. Angela did not have her own lawyer. The school used a top law firm to conduct the investigation.

BIRCH (*beat*). That does seem to suggest something rather more than incompetence.

BEN. 'For my birthday, I wore my DKNY T-shirt with the plunging neckline... seventeen cupcakes from Lulu's... We played the 'Ave Maria' together. Every time I gave the cue, I leaned over so he could see down my shirt. Maybe he likes-*likes* me, as a man desires a woman?' How does that sound to you, Birch?

BIRCH. I wouldn't read too much into that. Girls use their diaries to fantasise all the time.

MERCY. I certainly did.

BEN. 'I wish I were a little African girl. I wish my body had been purged by FGM, that my sinful desiring part had been cut out of me when I was seven.' She felt pleasure. Then the guilt came crashing down. It was buyer's remorse. Not rape.

BIRCH. Even if she writhed around naked on his knee, he was still duty bound to restrain himself.

Scene Eight

February.

The admissions office.

ANGELA *knocks and enters without waiting for a reply.*

ANGELA. Hi, Mercy!

MERCY. Angela. I would appreciate it if you made an appointment first.

ANGELA. I emailed.

MERCY. It must have gone into spam. What can I do for you?

ANGELA. I borrowed a violin, and played the blues busker piece! I haven't been able to play since – you know…

MERCY. I'm very happy for you.

ANGELA. It's all because of you – it's the violinist, not the violin. Thank you so much.

MERCY. You've very welcome. Now if you'd excuse me –

ANGELA. But I still can't play my Bach aria.

MERCY. Which Bach aria?

ANGELA. My competition aria. The 'Have Mercy Upon Me' aria.

MERCY. Why don't you just change your piece to a Paganini or something.

ANGELA. I can't.

MERCY. You can change it once.

ANGELA. This Bach aria is like a mountain in my path. There's no way around it. I have to scale it. But every time I even think about playing it, I hear the violin part in an impossibly high register, mocking me, crushing me –

MERCY. Why don't you get professional help –

ANGELA. It's what I heard when he forced me on my knees.

MERCY. Stop.

ANGELA. When he grabbed my hair, when he pushed me down, when he undid his zip, the *stench*, the suffocation –

MERCY. You wanted it.

ANGELA. No.

MERCY. Don't lie to me, stop lying to me –

ANGELA. I'm telling the truth!

MERCY. You wanted the sinful desiring part cut out of your body.

ANGELA. You read my diary?

MERCY. How dare you trivialise, *appropriate* Female Genital Mutilation for some sick rape fantasy!

ANGELA. No!

MERCY. Did you feel pleasure? Yes or no?

ANGELA. I hate him!

MERCY. Yes or no.

ANGELA. I was so scared, he stank, it was gross, but he *forced* me to *feel… against my will* you've got to understand, he prided himself on – he did things to me – I can't even describe – his stubble like rough towels rubbing against my thighs – my body did things and felt things I could not stop –

MERCY. It's not tickling. A woman needs to feel some emotional – to feel safe. Loved. No one can force you to have an orgasm.

ANGELA. How would you know?

MERCY. You're reviving every cliché about women and rape – 'her lips say no but her cunt says yes' – You don't deserve the title of 'rape survivor'.

ANGELA. I never used that word. Good rape victims only feel pain and revulsion. That's why I'd never press charges though I hate him, I hate him, I hate him for what he did, I hate it that he did whatever he wanted to my body, I hate that I let him do it, I hate it most that my body responded.

MERCY. Shouldn't have seduced him at your little cupcake party then.

ANGELA. Cupcakes?

MERCY. From Lulu's.

ANGELA. He got the cupcakes. For my seventeenth birthday.

MERCY. You let him look down your shirt!

ANGELA. And I have paid. He shoved it up my butt that last time. I thought I was going to split in half, like the magician sawing the woman in two but for real. He came. I curled up in a ball. He went down on me, and I came and came and came. After that, for two weeks, every time I took a step, I felt such pain, but the pain made me want to come again. I know I've become a monster. My wires are twisted between pleasure and pain, love and hate. I'll never get married, have kids, be normal.

Pause.

MERCY (*slowly*). Your seventeenth birthday. How long had he been teaching you when you turned seventeen?

ANGELA. Four months.

MERCY. The age of consent is seventeen in New York State. Sex with a minor under seventeen is statutory rape.

Pause.

ANGELA. He waited until I turned seventeen.

Scene Nine

The lights dim. Voices representing alumni who report on their achievements, their failures and their disorientation.

A. We welcomed Carol Sibyl Blair to the world today. Her parents and four Eliot godparents are very proud!

B. Currently interning in China with the Nature Conservancy in Sichuan. Looking forward to a future that is as multilingual, multicultural, and spicy as my present!

C. Appointed Senior Vice President at the World Bank.

D. I am now a federal judge in Massachusetts.

A. After ten years in management consulting, I teach roller-blading in Central Park.

B. I'm thirty-five and still wondering what to do when I grow up.

C. I write to you from federal prison. I've been here since last October for mis-selling municipal bonds. Tutoring prisoners in English and statistics.

D. Ex-Lehman Brothers banker, driving an ice-cream van in New Jersey.

A. Current occupation – prisoner. Achievements – eight life sentences. Current address: No. 04475-046, US Penitentiary – Max –

This scene overlaps with...

Scene Ten

March.

Admissions office.

BIRCH *stands facing the audience.* BEN *and* MERCY *are seated with the audience.*

BIRCH (*reading from the alumni magazine, simultaneously with* B *from the last scene*). 'Current occupation – prisoner. Achievements – eight life sentences. Current address: No. 04475-046, US Penitentiary – Max.' (*Beat.*) Acceptance by Eliot is not a golden ticket to Willy Wonka's Chocolate Factory, it would seem. (*Beat.*) I know passions are running high. I know that the thirty cases we will discuss in full committee today have their champions and their detractors. I know there will be a desperate scrambling for the last five places. But let's remember we're not God. We are not Fate. And we will get some of it wrong. We think we're judging these young people, but perhaps it is we who are being judged. As individuals. As an institution. Mercy, if you would present the first case, Angela Chan –

MERCY *doesn't stir.*

Mercy – your floor.

MERCY. I have nothing to add.

BIRCH (*beat*). Very well then. Let's vote. Yays – ten – (*Puts up her hand.*) Nays.

BEN*'s hand shoots up.*

Eleven. Abstentions: fourteen. Mercy – is that an abstention?

Pause. MERCY *puts up her hand tentatively.*

Fifteen. Unless Angela Chan wins the music-scholarship competition next week, she is a rejection.

Scene Eleven

April. Afternoon.

Admissions office.

BIRCH. We can't possibly afford two air tickets plus accommodation for every accepted candidate.

BEN. These families believe Eliot to be an alien, hostile world. We've got to show them their kids are welcome, that they can *belong*. We're talking – how many here? Fifty possible candidates from rough inner-city neighbourhoods, and another fifty from Arkansas, Alabama, the Appalachian states –

MERCY. Redneck country. Breitbart country.

BEN. Class diversity is just as important as racial diversity, Mercy. So two hundred air tickets. Eliot can afford two hundred air tickets to fly in diverse candidates and their parents, and we're going to lay it on for them. I want the parents put up in the Eliot guest house. I want each candidate to be paired up with a student from a similar background. I want each family to get a free Boston City pass. I want the families to feel like we really want them here as well, that we're not going to take their sons and daughters and turn them into unrecognisable snobs after four years.

BIRCH. We don't have the budget for it. I'm sorry.

BEN. Yale's doing it. Stanford's doing it. Princeton is flying out both parents of the candidates they most want.

BIRCH. We can continue this discussion later. Shall we?

BEN. What?

BIRCH. It's almost time for the music-scholarship competition.

BEN. Afraid I'm going to have to take a rain-check.

BIRCH. You're a music professor.

BEN. And I've got to call the mother of a black jazz pianist in Baltimore. She doesn't think we're offering her daughter enough financial aid.

BEN *exits*.

BIRCH. Mercy?

MERCY. I'm meeting with a Native American lacrosse player.

Knocking at the door.

BIRCH *answers the door.*

ANGELA *is at the door with her violin. She is wearing a blue evening dress.*

Oh hello, Angela.

ANGELA. Good afternoon, Dr Coffin.

MERCY *packs up her stuff and leaves.*

BIRCH. The competition is in Paine Hall.

ANGELA *enters. She catches a glimpse of the departing* MERCY.

ANGELA. I'm not playing.

BIRCH. Are you still struggling to play?

ANGELA. No. I choose not to play.

BIRCH (*beat*). Just to be clear – you will be forfeiting your last chance of getting into Eliot.

ANGELA. I've been accepted at Yale and Stanford.

BIRCH. But did you get enough financial aid from them?

Pause. The answer is no.

Angela, you could forfeit any possibility of staying on in this country

ANGELA (*derisively*). 'Life, liberty and the pursuit of happiness'?

BIRCH. So what will you do?

ANGELA. You think I can't just walk away from it all?

BIRCH. You have come dressed to play. (*Beat.*) Very well then. I shall go and withdraw your name from the competition.

BIRCH *moves towards the exit.*

ANGELA. How does the Mercy aria start? With a violin solo too high for the human voice to reach, phrases too long for

human lungs to sustain, ornamentation too intricate...
The singer tries so hard to copy the melody but can't. It's
mocking, it's derisive, it's crushing...

BIRCH. But the violin solo is propelled by that 12/8 walking
bass – those tears flowing down Peter's cheeks. That divine
glory is not indifferent to our pain.

ANGELA. In Hong Kong I was a Ming vase, mute, polished,
ornamental, but there was an honesty to that. No one ever
said I was a great artiste, a unique talent; no one took my
hand and promised me the keys to paradise.

Beat.

Do you know what Bach did with his music? His boy
choristers sang his 'Matthew Passion' to condemned
criminals en route to the gallows. He stood me up against the
back of a sofa and made me play Bach. I played with all my
heart, with all my strength; I prayed for a miracle – for an
angel with flaming sword to stop him... but all the angel did
was crush me...

BIRCH. So play that.

ANGELA. What?

BIRCH. Play it angry. Ugly. Broken.

ANGELA. How can I possibly play anything after this? There's
nothing left. I could play at Carnegie Hall, I could play with
the Berlin Philharmonic, I could win Grammy awards and at
the end of the day still just be a body to be used by men,
abused by men. You know and I know that's what the world
sees when it sees me. (*Beat.*) Isn't that what you see?

BIRCH. No. I bet that if you play, you'll find you've not been
abandoned. That broken voice – isn't it absolutely supported
from above and below? That violin solo is a promise that even
at the breaking point, when you feel utterly abandoned, utterly
alone, there's always someone to accompany you on your
path. When your breath runs out, when your song's about to
die, there's a violin there to catch you and complete the song.

Both ANGELA *and* BIRCH *hear the 'Mercy' aria in its full
glory – (bars 15–23, the violin/voice duet).*

Scene Twelve

May.

BIRCH *is packing up the contents of her desk into boxes.*

MERCY *enters.*

Pause.

MERCY. I still don't understand why you are leaving. Why now? There's so much to do, so many pieces to pick up – the new guidelines on mental health, the new sexual-harassment procedures... What will you do?

BIRCH. Thirty years ago, my father forbade me the study of theology because he thought women couldn't be clergy. I am enrolling at Yale Divinity School. (*Beat.*) I hope you are staying. Good luck.

BIRCH *has finished packing and puts on her light spring coat.*

MERCY. I just felt she needed a fresh start.

BIRCH. Who?

MERCY. Angela Chan. (*Beat.*) Manchester is a great city. (*Beat.*) We don't really have the resources to support someone so traumatised... (*Beat.*) She played like she was at war – she's obviously deeply disturbed. I'm surprised she got second. That was – whatever that was, it wasn't Bach.

BIRCH. You were there?

MERCY. I sneaked in. I was at the back. Just couldn't stay away.

Pause.

BEN *enters.*

BEN. Birch! I just want to say – thank you so much for all you've done here. Whatever I go on to achieve in this role, I'm very much aware it's because I stand on the shoulders of a giant.

BIRCH. Thank you.

BIRCH *leaves.*

BEN *goes to his desk, and takes out a bottle of champagne and two glasses. He pours and hands* MERCY *a glass.*

BEN. Cheers!

BEN *drains a glass.*

MERCY. Are you drinking to Birch's resignation?

BEN. I've just spoken to our lawyers – you're permanent now. The visa too.

MERCY. Thank you.

BEN. Where would I be without my right-hand woman?

What's wrong?

MERCY. Nothing. I just have a migraine.

BEN (*moving closer*). Acupressure?

MERCY (*backing away*). I just need to lie down in a dark room. (*Beat.*) How did you know she was gorgeous?

BEN. What?

MERCY. Angela Chan. You said don't underestimate the pressure a gorgeous young girl can put on a man. How did you know she was gorgeous?

BEN. You told me.

MERCY. No I didn't.

BEN. Birch must have told me. What does it matter anyway.

Pause.

MERCY. See you tomorrow, Professor Cohen... Dean Cohen.

Scene Thirteen

Fifteen months ago.

Foyer of Lincoln Centre, New York City.

ANGELA *is in a blue evening dress. She has her violin with her. She's lining up at the bar.*

BEN *enters and stands next to* ANGELA.

BEN. Chocolate or vanilla?

ANGELA. I'm sorry?

BEN. Do you like chocolate ice cream, or vanilla? Or perhaps you like raspberry sorbet –

ANGELA. Green tea.

BEN. The line for hot beverages is over there.

ANGELA. I like green-tea ice cream.

BEN. Why not. There I am, the blundering American –

ANGELA. No worries.

BEN. Schubert or Schumann?

ANGELA. What?

BEN. Would you prefer to meet Schubert or Schumann – say at a bar?

ANGELA. Schumann was insane. Schubert had syphilis. Definitely Schumann.

They laugh.

BEN. I like that. Who's your favourite Muppet?

ANGELA. Kermit.

BEN. The voice of idealism. With a sense of irony. Have you seen the Kermit Klein ads?

ANGELA. No.

BEN. Oh they're utterly hilarious. You've seen those Calvin Klein ads with Marky Mark?

ANGELA. Yes...

BEN. Kermit Klein is a spoof.

ANGELA. So a moodily lit Kermit –

BEN. Black and white, very classy –

ANGELA. With his briefs sticking out of his jeans?

BEN. You bet.

ANGELA. Miss Piggy must be delighted –

BEN. Yup. No prizes for guessing what she's doing in her panties – ah sorry sorry. Look I don't think they've quite caught up to green-tea ice cream here. Can I get you strawberry?

ANGELA. No I'm fine. Thanks.

BEN. A drink? Oooh look at this, a green-tea mojito!

ANGELA. I don't have ID.

BEN (*mock-grandiosely*). She's with me. Cocktail for the lady, please. On the rocks.

ANGELA *giggles*.

ANGELA. I don't think we have time before the second half begins.

BEN. Do we have to go back in?

ANGELA. I felt very – disturbed too. Midori plays like she's at war –

BEN. Don't blame you. I remember when Midori was a dainty Japanese elf of a child prodigy. She's really let herself go.

ANGELA. You don't worry about your looks when you're struggling with the angel.

BEN. You've lost me there.

ANGELA. She plays Bach like it's a dark labyrinth, concealing a divinity in its heart.

BEN. I'd love to hear you play.

ANGELA. I could be terrible.

BEN. I doubt it.

A bell rings. The PA system announces that the concert will commence again in five minutes.

ANGELA *gets up.*

Say we have fifty grand to consume tonight – *consume*, all of it, tonight, so no buying of property, no investment, no giving away to charity – what would you do?

ANGELA. That's easy.

BEN. You think?

ANGELA. I would hire Carnegie Hall, and the Gibson Stradivarius –

BEN. The one stolen from the dressing room of Carnegie Hall?

ANGELA. Then sold to a hack musician who played it in restaurants for the next fifty years. No one noticed.

BEN. The thief confesses on his deathbed, and Joshua Bell buys the Strad.

ANGELA. He busks like a hobo in the Washington metro –

BEN. A superstar violinist, playing Bach on a Stradivarius during morning rush hour –

ANGELA. Seven people stopped –

BEN. Thirty-two dollars in tips. A total flop!

ANGELA. Do you really think so? You never know who receives the music. And seven people stopped.

BEN. I love your passion. (*Beat.*) So what would you do once you have this incognito Stradivarius in Carnegie Hall? I can see you there, charming the pants off everyone, cameras lapping you up, glowing alabaster in your blue dress, like a Ming vase –

ANGELA. It's not Ming blue.

BEN. It's a lovely shade –

ANGELA. It's ultramarine.

BEN. Aha! A fan of Renaissance painting –

ANGELA. Rembrandt.

BEN (*confused*). A Rembrandt blue?

ANGELA. There is no blue in Rembrandt.

BEN (*beat*). You're right. He doesn't really venture beyond yellow in the colour spectrum. I never noticed. Why?

ANGELA. There is no heaven in Rembrandt.

BEN. There is no heaven in Rembrandt. Fascinating. You have a beautiful mind. I usually try to make MetFridays. Any chance of seeing you there?

ANGELA. What's MetFridays?

BEN. The Metropolitan Museum of Art is open late every Friday evening. You from out of town?

ANGELA (*embarrassed*). No. Yes. I just got here.

BEN. From where?

ANGELA. Hong Kong.

BEN. Wow. Fresh off the plane!

ANGELA. You think I'm provincial?

BEN. Not at all. You're passionate and sophisticated and – ultramarine – that's the colour of the Virgin Mary, isn't it?

ANGELA. Yes.

A moment.

BEN. And what brings you to New York City?

ANGELA. I got a scholarship to the Performing Arts High School.

BEN. I teach there once a week! (*Beat.*) So I will get to hear you play…

Pause.

The bell rings, summoning the audience.

What's your name?

ANGELA. Angela.

The End.

www.nickhernbooks.co.uk

facebook.com/nickhernbooks

twitter.com/nickhernbooks